Captive in Norway

The True Story of One American
Family's Fight to Recover Their
Stolen Children from Norway's
Child Welfare Service Agency

by

Samantha Harrell

"*Captive in Norway* is a wake-up call for families who are considering travelling to Norway. I would highly recommend reading this heartbreaking and excellent account that details every step of how three innocent children were needlessly and violently abducted from their loving American family. Read it, share, and pray for the reunification and healing for these children and their family!"
— **Steven Bennett**
Author of Stolen Childhood: The Truth about Norway's Child Welfare System

"When I started reading *Captive in Norway*, I couldn't put it down. It broke my heart for this family and made me angry with the justice system around the world. I wonder why those in governmental leadership in the US have made excuses instead of helping, and this book gave me the urge to keep fighting against the injustice. I was left feeling hopeful that there will be justice for this family and that they will be back as a family unit soon. Samantha Harrell does an excellent job telling Natalya's story, sharing the heart of this mother fighting to get her children back home. She is a beautiful writer and draws her audience to desire to want to be part of the bigger solution."
— **Judi Riccio**
Executive Director of Faithful Love, Inc., an organization that works with adult survivors of sex trafficking

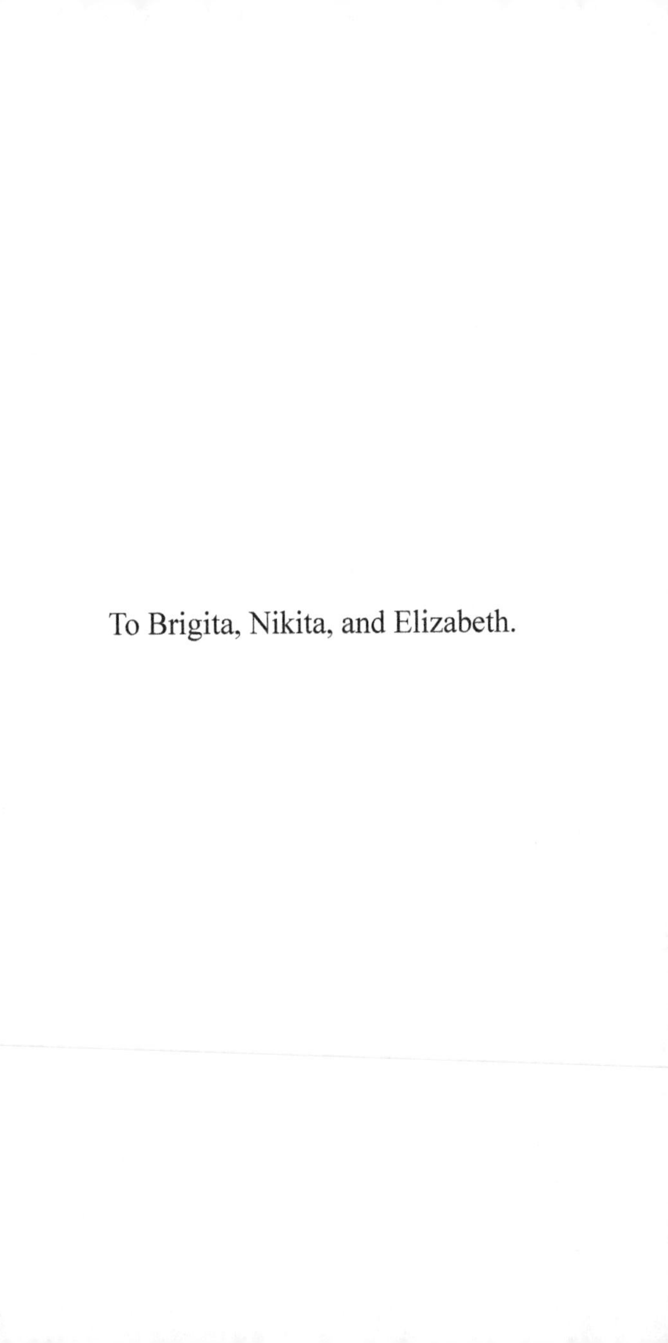

To Brigita, Nikita, and Elizabeth.

Contents

Foreword

Natalya and Zyg,

First, let me say how thankful I am that the Lord let us cross paths. We have come to cherish you and truly consider you our friends. We are been shocked to see the treatment you have received and how brutal the system has been against you. Your situation is truly an example that calls for change in our country.

I am thankful for all our conversations, and I pray for many more as the children are returned. I pray that those involved see what they have done and change for the better. To think these people know your children better than yourselves after 144 days in Norway is a disgrace—and I hope for an aftermath in this case. I also urge those still caught in this system to not stay silent. Think differently; write a timeline, take notes of everything that could have been done differently, and to not be afraid. Remember that you are teaching those around you at all times. The general population cannot imagine the cruelty that is happening: make them listen.

My heart trembles when I recall our first meeting—seeing you physically work through the pain of having your kids robbed from you in a foreign country. The worst of it all was the lack of helping hands: Where were your neighbors? Where were the kind souls who were supposed to help you? I have never experienced this level of disappointment before—not only from our government, its lack of understanding and caring, but also from the community that didn't respond. Our politicians that never responded. The municipal leadership who just referred to the courts. People who assumed you were guilty, despite not knowing who you were. That is by far the evidence to show that we ourselves drive injustice.

From that critical moment, when the pain was the deepest, I have seen you both rise above this evil with such grace, understanding, and wisdom. When suffering came, you said you turned back to God—and clung to hope.

Thank you Natalya and Zyg for your smiles, even in times when you didn't feel like smiling. You never yielded or gave up hope. You were firm in the truth. I love you deeply and will always be here for you and your family. You are an inspiration to all of us.

Sincerely,

Katrine Stangelo

Introduction

"The moment you step your foot in this socialist country, your kid belongs to the government, not to you—harsh truth. I can barely speak when asked about my stolen children. I feel like I'm broken. My voice starts shaking, and I start crying. I'm way too emotional about it—still. Seven months after moving to Norway, our life crumbled. Everything we had worked so hard for, for so many years, was gone within minutes. I kept thinking that when I woke up, the nightmare would be over. That I'd get to wake the kids up for school again—but it didn't happen. I walked through empty rooms, crying uncontrollably, howling like a wolf. I couldn't find comfort and had no peace of mind. So I turned to God. I prayed. I asked my family and

> my church back in Atlanta to pray.
> We're all still praying to this day."

It's the last thing one would expect to hear from a mother of three beautiful children, but this was Natalya Shutakova's message to me on Tuesday, August 25, 2020. Natalya does not live with all of her children, only with her husband, Zigintas Aleksandravicius, and their youngest child, Elizabeth. The couple had lived in Notodden, Norway, since September 1, 2018, when they moved there from Atlanta, Georgia, with their young children. For more than two years, all three their children, Brigita (age thirteen), Nikita (age twelve), and Elizabeth (age nine), lived at three separate, secret Norwegian foster homes. So far, only Elizabeth has been returned to Natalya and Zigintas, whose nickname is Zygys. Brigita and Nikita rarely see their parents since they were abducted by the child "protective services" division of the Norwegian government on May 20, 2019.

The family enjoyed a happy life in the United States, where all three children were born and raised as American citizens. Zygys and Natalya met in Atlanta in 2007. She was a naturalized US citizen, having lived in the country since age eleven. He had lived in the US since age twenty-six and was in the country on a visa. After meeting, the couple moved to Miami, where they lived six years and had their two eldest children. The family then moved back to Atlanta, where their baby girl was born in 2012, and where they lived six more years. Zygys traveled for work as a remodeling contractor, while Natalya stayed home with her little ones.

In June of 2018, the family left the United States for Lithuania, Zygys' country of birth, to renew his visa. Natalya thought it best to accompany him with the children, as he was unsure when he could return to the US. He began applying for jobs in many European countries, and a month later, he received a contract to work in Oslo, Norway. Zygys went ahead of his family to Norway, where he worked for two months before Natalya and the children joined him there in August at their new home in Notodden. The children started at their new Norwegian school on September 1, 2018, knowing no one and struggling to learn the language.[1]

---

1. Shutakova, N. (2020). (S. Harrell, Interviewer)

Norway has not been kind to this wonderful family. They are the victims of modern human trafficking under the incredibly insidious guise of child protection. This is the story of their faith and hope in God when the odds appear to be stacked against them and when the devil's lies say all hope is lost. Much of this book is written as the family's story unfolds; details were added to the book as the events happened. In September 2020, my research caught up to and collided with real life in the courtroom. Prior to that date, I scrolled through months of Natalya's social media posts, searching for clues, photographs, dates, and links. I messaged her with questions and encouragement, and she graciously responded with her memories and frustrations.

As you read their story, please stop occasionally and pray for Natalya's family. It might sound something like this:

> Dear Lord Jesus, please return Brigita, Nikita, and Elizabeth to their parents swiftly and safely. Please keep them at peace and safe from harm as you masterfully unravel the trap they are caught in. Give them victory in the courts and even in the rare family

meetings they are allowed. Show your power in all of these situations so their tormentors will know the Almighty God and repent, come to know you, and be saved. We know they are part of a nefarious system that preys on and traps the innocent and vulnerable. Please disable the wicked Barnevernet system so that no one else has to suffer like Natalya's family. Replace the corrupt child welfare and protective institutions throughout the world with organizations that have your heart for families and children. Bring this nightmare to an end for Natalya's family, as well as for another American family, Tyler and Amy Jakobsen, who have also been separated by Barnevernet. Please restore these families and all they have lost and more. In your holy name, I pray, Amen.

> *God will do this, for he is*
> *faithful to do what he says,*
> *and he has invited you into*
> *partnership with his Son,*
> *Jesus Christ our Lord.*
> 1 Corinthians 1:9 (NLT)

May 2019

May 17th is a "National Day" in Norway, an annual reminder of the country's independence from Sweden. Norway's constitution was signed on this day in 1814. Each year Norwegians of all ages take to the streets for this celebration, known as "syttende mai," in traditional dress ("bunad") to march in parades and freely consume junk food such as ice cream and hot dogs, as well as fish or porridge, depending on the region.[2] It is quite a happy celebration, complete with the national flag, marching bands, and even an appearance by Oslo's royal family. People are heard greeting each other with, "Gratulerer med dagen!" It means "congratulations with the day," or "happy birthday," referring to Norway's birthday in 1814.

Brigita Shutakova was at this birthday celebration with her family in Notodden, Norway,

---

2. More than a National Day: Understanding May 17th of Norway. (n.d.), The Nordic Page.

on Friday, May 17, 2019. She beamed as she held the Norwegian flag while wearing a beautiful black-and-white dress and eating ice cream. It was her birthday, too, and an exciting start to a festive weekend celebrating with her family. Things could not have been better for Brigita, for she had just turned eleven and received a new smartphone from her parents.[3] The city's beautiful flowers and scenic view served as the perfect backdrop for her special day, as she smiled for photographs with her little brother, younger sister, and parents. It must have seemed as if the city had thrown a big party just for her.

Brigita's birthday celebration continued through the weekend. On Sunday, May 19, she and her family traveled to Drammen, Norway, to sit atop the Drammen Spiral tunnel and take in the surrounding views.[4] The helix-shaped tunnel was formed while tunneling for stone. It opened in 1961 as a route for vehicle travel up to Skansen Ridge. Vehicles ascend the rising spiral and go around in six circles until finally coming to rest at

---

3. Shutakova, N. (2019, June 6). Podcast Episode 14 - Three American Children Brutally Taken by Norway's Dysfunctional CPS.

4. Korf, B. (2019, June 13), Three American children brutally ripped from their beds at night in Norway, Step Up 4 Children's Rights.

the top where visitors can eat at the café and admire the surrounding beauty. The same day, Brigita and her family also explored Oslo, Norway's capital city.

At some point that Sunday, Brigita's parents decided it would be best to temporarily relieve Brigita of her new cell phone in hopes of improving the child's behavior. As might be expected of a girl her age with such an irresistible new "toy," she had abused her privileges with it over the weekend by overusing it, and her parents believed she needed a break from it. Additionally, her parents made it clear to Brigita that if her behavior did not improve, she would not have a birthday party with friends.[5] Understandably, Brigita became angry and harbored resentment until the next day at school.[6]

Back at school Monday, Brigita was not her usual cheerful self. Her teacher found it suspicious that she was in such poor spirits so soon after her birthday weekend, so she questioned Brigita about what was wrong.[7] Because she

---

5.Shutakova, N. (2020, May 20), (E. Metaxas, Interviewer).

6. Bonanza Media. (Director). (2019). American Children Lost to Norway [Motion Picture].

7. Shutakova, N. (2019, June 6). Podcast Episode 14 - Three American Children Brutally Taken by Norway's Dysfunctional CPS.

was angry with her parents for taking her cell phone, and in an effort to get back at them, Brigita complained falsely to her teachers about being hungry and not getting lunch. Apparently, she also falsely accused her parents of "some violence" or physical mistreatment at home.[8]

Her teacher called Natalya to ask why Brigita did not have food and even said it wasn't the first time Brigita had "gone hungry with no lunch." The teacher also claimed to have given Brigita food from the teacher's cafeteria on previous similar occasions. Confused, Natalya drove to the school, as she was sure Brigita went to school with lunch in her backpack. Upon arriving, Natalya found the lunch hidden in her backpack.[9] Brigita confessed to lying and expressed concern that her parents would ground her.[10] If only that could have served as her punishment! That afternoon, Brigita and her parents discussed her lie about not having lunch, but according to Natalya, "there was no thorough talk. None

8. Bonanza Media. (Director). (2019). American Children Lost to Norway [Motion Picture].

9. Shutakova, N. (2019, June 6). Podcast Episode 14 - Three American Children Brutally Taken by Norway's Dysfunctional CPS.

10. Shutakova, N. (2020, February 28), (J. V. Maren, Interviewer).

of us knew it was going to be our last talk about right and wrong."[11]

Natalya tucked the three children into their beds at home that same night around 8:00 p.m. She and their father, Zygys, were still up watching TV on the sofa at 9:00 p.m. when they noticed police cars outside. Natalya opened the door, and multiple Norwegian police officers entered the apartment. Accompanying the police was a member of the notorious Norwegian Child Protection Service, or "Barnevernet." One of the officers stated in broken English, "You have been accused of child mistreatment. Your daughter has complained in school about some violence." With no further explanation, the unwelcome group entered their home "as if it were theirs" and walked right into the children's bedrooms. The officers startled them from their sleep and bullied them into compliance, ordering them outside. Although Natalya was not allowed to speak to the children as they were being kidnapped, the children managed to give their parents goodbye hugs and kisses. Only Brigita, the eldest, could understand what was happening. The entire family was

---

11. Shutakova, N. (2020). (S. Harrell, Interviewer)

apprehended and driven to the police station in Skien for questioning.[12]

At the station, each member of the family was interrogated alone for three hours with no translation into English or Russian and no family attorney was permitted.[13] Natalya and Zygys understood when asked if they spanked the children that it is illegal in Norway.[14] Finally, the children were loaded into separate vehicles and driven straight to different, secret foster homes around Norway. As with so many other government child-abductions in Norway, there had been no warning, no offers of help, and no investigation or hearing prior to this horrific and heartbreaking home invasion and kidnapping.[15] According to Natalya, the victims of these situations are never allowed to have witnesses or representation during the interrogation. It's usually just the victim's word against that of the Barnevernet employees and their state psychologists, who are allowed to be present

---

12.Shutakova, N. (2020). (S. Harrell, Interviewer)

13. Flory, N. (2019, October 10), The American-Born Kidnapped Children of Norway, The Stream.

14. Smith, S. (2019, July 3), 3 American children removed from parents' home by Norway's child services, The Christian Post.

15. Korf, B. (2019, June 13), Three American children brutally ripped from their beds at night in Norway, Step Up 4 Children's Rights.

during interrogations, resulting in courtroom wins for the state nearly every time.[16]

Shortly after the interrogations, the Norwegian police opened a criminal case against Zygys and Natalya. The couple was jailed for twenty-four hours and only released after signing a "no-contact" form[17] and agreeing not to contact their own children until June 11th, which was supposed to be their first supervised meeting together.[18] Barnevernet claimed to need that time to conduct their own investigation.[19] The parents were threatened with a two-year prison penalty if these terms were violated. These bogus threats and agreements were likely just an underhanded way for Barnevernet to ensure the parents and children do not seek help from each other or others who might be able to intervene early and undermine their plan to transport and imprison the children in secret foster homes. The parents are immediately

16. Smith, S. (2019, July 3), 3 American children removed from parents' home by Norway's child services, The Christian Post.

17. Shutakova, N. (2020, May 20), (E. Metaxas, Interviewer).

18. Shutakova, N. (2019, June 6). Podcast Episode 14 - Three American Children Brutally Taken by Norway's Dysfunctional CPS.

19. Korf, B. (2019, June 13), Three American children brutally ripped from their beds at night in Norway, Step Up 4 Children's Rights.

bullied into silence, while the best course of action would actually be to raise awareness through various media outlets and hire a private investigator, if possible. Contacting the authorities with jurisdiction is always the first step in the case of a missing person,[20] but of course, this cannot apply when the authorities are the instigators.

20. Kay, L. J. (2020, April 14), Don't Wait to Report a Missing Person, The Enterprise.

Summer 2019

Elizabeth, the youngest daughter in the family, turned seven on June 7, 2019.[21] Sadly, this was also the date when a Norwegian court, after hearing the family's case for the first time on June 6th, ruled that the three children would remain in temporary foster care. The ruling promised that the family would be allowed to meet together once a week for an hour, beginning June 11th. When that date rolled around, however, "the parents were informed that they cannot see their children, as the Barnevernet and police want to do further interrogations with them separately."[22] This cruelty would prove typical of the secular Barnevernet, which has little to no oversight and seems to care nothing for the children it purports to protect.

21. Shutakova, N. (2019, June 6). Podcast Episode 14 - Three American Children Brutally Taken by Norway's Dysfunctional CPS.

22. Korf, B. (2019, June 13), Three American children brutally ripped from their beds at night in Norway, Step Up 4 Children's Rights.

The family's attorneys appealed to the court shortly afterward for more visitation, and Natalya and Zygys were permitted to meet with their two youngest, Nikita and Elizabeth, on June 19th. This began a series of weekly, two-hour supervised visits with the children. Barnevernet sent their translator to be present to eavesdrop and report back about the conversations between the children and their parents. Nonetheless, the children were thrilled to see their parents each week, showering them with hugs and kisses, and crying once their happy time together was over. According to Natalya, "It was very painful to let them go every time, to relive, again and again, that trauma of separation. Every Friday was 'thank God you guys are here,' and then two hours later, that trauma was there again for everybody, the kids and us, the parents."[23]

In May 2019, immediately after her children were abducted, Natalya discovered Step Up 4 Children's Rights, a group of Christian parents in Vienna, Austria, who have organized to speak up for all the children stolen from the parents by Norwegian authorities. The group works with the relevant attorneys, politicians,

---

23. Shutakova, N. (2020, February 15), (B. Korf, Interviewer).

and psychologists to spread awareness and work toward victims' rescue. Step Up 4 Children's Rights regularly publishes interviews and case updates through social media, internet video, and podcasts, and has recently published a book on the subject titled *Stolen Childhood.*

In this case, the organization's first action was to notify Natalya's home church in Atlanta, Georgia. Bjorn Korf, the group's co-founder, asked the church to use social media to stand up for the family, including covering them with prayer. On June 25th, Step Up 4 Children's Rights aired a podcast interview with Natalya titled "Norway Seized Our Kids." On June 28th, the organization published an online petition directed to American Vice President Mike Pence, asking him to investigate the situation and demand to see Norway's evidence of parental abuse. Natalya feels that this organization has been in her corner since day one. God's compassion, truth, and desire for justice is evident in the shocking information that His messengers from Step Up 4 Children's Rights have so bravely broadcasted to the world.

The entire family was reunited briefly on Friday, June 28th, the same day Step Up 4 Children's Rights published their first petition. Natalya and Zygys were allowed to see all three children at once.[24] It was an emotionally mixed reunion. The children were elated to be with their parents but cried when the short visit was over. Brigita apologized to her parents for accusing them of mistreatment and begged Barnevernet to let her go home. "[Brigita] said she is sorry for all the things she said; she didn't mean to say that. She regrets everything. [Barnevernet] was present when our oldest was saying she has made the worst mistake in her life."[25] Barnevernet replied that the children must be traumatized from seeing their parents.[26] The truth is that the damage is Barnevernet's fault completely for compounding the trauma of another separation on top of the first. As Natalya puts it:

> I know my kids better than anyone, and I sure know they are not challenged. What this system has done to

24. Shutakova, N. (2020, February 28), (J. V. Maren, Interviewer).

25. Smith, S. (2019, July 3), 3 American children removed from parents' home by Norway's child services, The Christian Post.

26. Flory, N. (2019, October 10), The American-Born Kidnapped Children of Norway, The Stream.

them made them traumatized. If they find it hard to manage my kids, they never should have taken them. But they never admit to causing distress to a child; it's always the parents' fault.[27]

By July 2019, two major Christian news outlets in the US picked up the story of Brigita, Nikita, and Elizabeth. First, the Christian Post published an article, noting that when the American Embassy in Oslo was notified about the case, they simply advised the family to "cooperate with Barnevernet and work with their lawyers."[28] Later in the month, CBN News published an eye-opening article titled "Norwegian Nightmare." The article explains that foreign families seem to be targeted, and details the similarly heartbreaking cases of other families who moved to Norway from Canada, Romania, and the US. Reasons for these child removals are as frivolous as "Christian indoctrination," homeschooling, and in the case of Amy Jakobsen, her one-year-old Tyler was one pound underweight.

---

27. Shutakova, N. (2020). (S. Harrell, Interviewer)

28. Smith, S. (2019, July 3), 3 American children removed from parents' home by Norway's child services, The Christian Post.

As a result of their abuses, Norway's Barnevernet has become infamous internationally, with twenty-six cases pending before the European Court of Human Rights as of July 2019. Their system has also been labeled as a front for human trafficking, as "billions and billions of dollars are being put into this system each year." The CBN article concludes that the US has yet to step up and help Natalya's family or the Jakobsens. It also includes a lengthy response from Norwegian State Secretary Jorunn Hallaraker to CBN News, outlining the measures Norway is taking to "improve" child welfare services. The secretary's response to CBN News actually appears to be a defense of the current system. It even boasts of continual increases in staff capacity and "competence development" in their incredibly young employees (who often have no experience with children of their own), rather than conceding the necessary system overhaul or disassembly.[29]

On August 7, 2019, the Norwegian police in Skien closed the criminal case against Natalya and her husband. Their investigation failed to produce evidence of child abuse,

29. Hurd, D. (2019, July 17), Norwegian Nightmare: 'Barnevernet' Preys On Children and Parents, CBN News.

only inconsistencies in the accusations.[30] Afterward, however, the children remained in captivity at their foster homes because Barnevernet disregarded the police investigation. Natalya commented, "The Norwegian CPS (child protective services) thinks they're above the law. But we have God on our side, so in this case, it will be victory."[31] The police went on to open a second and third case against Natalya and Zygys, both of which were closed.[32]

Interestingly, the US government came swiftly to the aid of American rapper A$AP Rocky after he found himself in a Swedish prison on assault charges in a Stockholm street brawl that took place on June 30, 2019. After pressure from various celebrities, President Trump and his envoy for hostage affairs demanded that Sweden release A$AP "as soon as possible to avoid potentially negative consequences to the US-Swedish bilateral relationship." Trump even offered to "personally vouch for his bail." A$AP was released

30. Bonanza Media. (Director). (2019). American Children Lost to Norway [Motion Picture].

31. Smith, S. (2019, August 10), Norwegian police drop criminal case against US family, but kids remain in CPS custody, The Christian Post.

32. Shutakova, N. (2020, May 20), (E. Metaxas, Interviewer).

from prison and returned to the US quickly thereafter, with his entire ordeal lasting just a little over a month.[33]

The US government immediately put the full force of its sway behind the rescue of an adult facing real assault charges so he wouldn't have to languish in a foreign prison. In the meantime, just hours away from that dramatic rescue, at least four innocent American children have been held captive for many months in abusive foster homes with no pressure from the US government to return them to their parents. That is inexcusable.

Meanwhile, Step Up 4 Children's Rights continued their tireless work for Brigita, Nikita, and Elizabeth. On August 26, 2019, the organization published a second online petition directed to the Norwegian Ambassadors in Berlin, Vienna, and Bern, as well as to Norway's Family & Children Minister, Mr. Kjell Ingolf Ropstad.

---

33. Givetash, L. (2019, August 3), A$AP Rocky Released from Swedish Jail, Back in the US., NBC News.

Fall 2019

On September 7, 2019, grassroots organizers demonstrated across Europe, including outside the Norwegian embassy in Oslo. The protesters called for an end to Barnevernet ideology in European child protection policy. Interestingly, the protests were initiated by Bulgarians, who are unhappy about the corrupt policies migrating to their country all the way from Norway: "The new concept and ideology were heavily promoted in Bulgaria through Norwegian grants." Norway seems to be behind the spread of this disease all over Europe, as many of the protests in other countries were held outside Norwegian embassies and consulates.[34]

Just three days later, on September 10th, Norway was convicted before the European Court of Human Rights based on Barnevernet's abusive treatment of another family,

34. International Protest: "STOP Barnevernet Ideology" in child protection laws. (2019, September 4), Family News.

Trude Lobben and her son. He was removed from her care more than a decade ago, and just one month after birth, when she naively went to Barnevernet for help as a single mother. Although Norway was found guilty of disrespecting the family's right to private and family life, they refused to remove the child from his adoptive parents and reunite him with his mother.[35]

God willing, Norway's rogue efforts to undermine God's natural family structure will be their undoing, as word of this evil continues to spread internationally.

Similarly, while the international "Black Lives Matter" movement does not have its roots in Norway, it shares a common goal: to "disrupt the nuclear family." Once this aim was highly publicized in the US, the BLM organization removed that language from its website.[36] Darkness does not want its true nature to remain uncovered and exposed.

---

35. Smith, S. (2019, October 5), Norway refuses to reunite mother with son despite victory at top European court, The Christian Post.

36. Miltimore, J. (2020, September 24), Black Lives Matter's Goal to 'Disrupt' the Nuclear Family Fits a Marxist Aim That Goes Back a Century and a Half, FEE.

The case of the Shutakova family was again heard in court at Skien, Norway, on September 17-18, 2019. This time, Natalya presented solid evidence against Barnevernet in the form of an online video in which Brigita confesses to lying about her parents, apologizes profusely, and pleads for help:

Today I am recording this video to any president. I want to explain what happened and why. Norway, I live here. It's pretty cool; it's beautiful. But the worst thing about it is that Norway separates families. My family got separated right after my birthday. I had a birthday on May 17th, and right after, we got separated. Barnevernet is stealing our families. They're separating our families, our children, everything that we love. I got separated May 20th because of some drama that happened. We were going on a vacation, that's when I got my phone, right after my birthday. We went to Oslo, the capital of Norway, and I was just stuck to my phone, like I won't take my eyes off of it. My mother and father told me to get my phone away. I was so addicted to it, and then they took my phone. And then the drama started and, because of me, my family got separated. I started some drama and I wasn't honest, and I made up some story, and I lied. I didn't know what I was doing. I lost control, I wasn't honest, I was so, so angry and I just made up a story. I just want to tell you guys, the president, that I am so sorry for my lying, but what I mostly want is I want my mom and dad back. My mom is Natalya Shutakova, and my dad is Zygys. My brother and sister are Nikita and Elizabeth. I really want them back.[37]

To bolster Brigita's confession, ten witnesses agreed that Brigita had been caught lying in the past. The witnesses also stated that they had never seen evidence of physical punishment of the children by their parents.[38] As a result, Barnevernet broke Brigita's cell phone

---

37. Hurd, D. (2019, September 27). 'Our Hearts Are Shattered': Norway Takes Permanent Custody of 3 American Children from Christian Parents, CBN News.

38. Flory, N. (2019, October 10), The American-Born Kidnapped Children of Norway, The Stream.

to prevent future video releases.[39] The Norwegian police even went so far as to confiscate Natalya's phones on November 26th, citing "potential kidnapping" of her own children as the reason.[40]

In response to the overwhelming evidence and witnesses in favor of reuniting the family, the Norwegian court ruled the Shutakova children would remain in foster care permanently. Barnevernet insisted the children did not have "proper rules or proper routine." Unfortunately, this, along with any other trumped-up reason fabricated by the child services caseworkers, is acceptable in Norwegian court as evidence of parental "neglect."[41] Natalya and Zygys were given three two-hour supervised visits per year, per child.[42] The dates and locations for meetings are chosen by Barnevernet. Natalya's son, Nikita, turned ten on October 8, 2019, in foster care. He was not permitted to visit

---

39. Hurd, D. (2019, September 27). 'Our Hearts Are Shattered': Norway Takes Permanent Custody of 3 American Children from Christian Parents, CBN News.

40. Shutakova, N. (2020). (S. Harrell, Interviewer)

41. Korf, B. (2019, June 13), Three American children brutally ripped from their beds at night in Norway, Step Up 4 Children's Rights.

42. Bonanza Media. (Director). (2019). American Children Lost to Norway [Motion Picture].

with his family, nor could he receive gifts or phone calls. These draconian rules and subjective standards of Norwegian parenting are levied against perfectly good families to legally trap and traffick their children into the lucrative foster care system. Sadly, Barnevernet refused to take action against Brigita's foster father when she reported to the police in August of 2019 that he threw her off of a bed and dragged her by the hair for refusing food.[43] Often, the corrupt agency turns a blind eye to actual abuse by the foster parents to focus on framing and punishing the innocent biological families.

On November 6, 2019, Bjorn Korf of Step Up 4 Children's Rights published an open, online letter to the US Embassy in Oslo asking for justice and assistance. The letter informs the officials that Natalya and Zygys have appealed to the US consulate for assistance—which they haven't received. It goes on to remind them that the Shutakova children and Tyler Jakobsen are still missing, kept as prisoners at secret addresses in Norway. The letter states: "[Natalya and Zigintas] have evidence that the children are suffering horrible physical and mental abuse

---

43. Shutakova, N. (2020). (S. Harrell, Interviewer)

while being in foster care. The Norwegian authorities won't release those children. It is very obvious that in both cases, several articles of the UN convention on the rights of the child were heavily violated." The plea concludes by requesting justice for the children from the US State Department and includes a reminder that kidnapping foreign citizens is a "serious act of war."[44]

This case continues to be largely ignored by the US government, despite continued requests for assistance from the Shutakova family and others who are concerned. It should be noted that the US and Norway have an arrangement to share defense supplies. In 2018, both countries entered the Security of Supply Arrangement, allowing the US Department of Defense to "request priority delivery for DoD contracts, subcontracts or orders from companies in [Norway]." While significant, the agreement is just one example of Norway's close relationship with the US, a bond that is continually strengthened as the countries work together on many different

---

44. Korf, B. (2019, November 6). Open Letter to the US Embassy in Oslo, Step Up 4 Children's Rights.

issues.[45] It may come as no surprise then that the US hesitates to intervene in private Norwegian matters of state, such as their defunct child protection service system.

45. Judson, J. (2018, April 12). US, Norway officially enter arrangement to share supplies for national security, *Defense News*

Winter 2019-2020

B arnevernet rejected Natalya's request for a holiday visit with her children, and so she and Zygys endured their first Christmas season without them.[46] On Christmas Day 2019, Bonanza Media released a short documentary online titled *American Children Lost to Norway*. The film presents a compelling interview with Natalya in which she describes Barnevernet's tactics and the aftermath of her family's separation:

> I met Zygys, love of my life, in Atlanta, Georgia, and we have three wonderful kids. Brigita, the oldest, she is now eleven. Nikita is ten, and our little princess Liza is seven. They're all American citizens; we had a pretty good life in America. A year ago, we moved to Norway because my husband has a work contract here. Never in a million years

---

46. Shutakova, N. (2020). (S. Harrell, Interviewer)

would I imagine that in just a few short months, we would be deprived of all our three children by Barnervernet, the so-called child protection service of Norway…Those two hours that you have, it's just not enough. It's nothing. The children come, and they don't know if they should be laughing or crying or going crazy; they're kids. Right now, the children are very traumatized. I see how traumatized they are…That's the trick; they don't want you to win. They will not let you win. Immediately after separation, they want your child to forget you. They don't work on reuniting the famly…I would ask Mr. Trump to please help my family get my children back to America. The children are American; they don't need to be here. They don't need to be placed with some strangers who don't even know how to speak with my children.[47]

Natalya's heartache is palpable and juxtaposed with scenes of the festive holiday atmosphere in Norway. However, the film makes

____

47. Bonanza Media. (Director). (2019). American Children Lost to Norway [Motion Picture].

it clear that she is not the only one suffering at the hands of Barnevernet during what should be a joyful time of year.

Barnevernet may aim to convince victimized parents that their children have forgotten them and are instead emotionally attached to their foster parents, but the evidence presented in *American Children Lost to Norway* proves that this couldn't be farther from the truth. The film highlights disturbing messages from Brigita, Natalya's eldest, suggesting she and her siblings are enduring a living nightmare of abuse apart from their God-given, loving parents. Brigita's suicide note to Natalya states that her foster carers "are the worst" and treat her like "sh*t." They even insist that Brigita refer to them as mommy and daddy. In a music video she made for Natalya, Brigita makes it painfully clear she is heartbroken and wants nothing more than to be reunited with her real mommy: "Mommy, my one and only mommy in the world, I dedicate this song to you. I love you a lot! I miss you! We will always be together. I love you!"[48]

---

48. Bonanza Media. (Director). (2019). American Children Lost to Norway [Motion Picture].

On February 28, 2020, Jonathan Van Maren aired an interview with Natalya that underscores her total frustration with the Norwegian government. She begins by explaining how, near the end of the summer in 2019, Barnevernet suddenly stopped allowing her to have weekly, two-hour visits with her children. The Norwegian police then opened a third criminal case against Natalya and Zygys. Only after snooping through Natalya's phones for two months did the police finally return them to her in January. They also attempted, unsuccessfully, to confiscate her and Zygys' passports. While all the bogus investigation found nothing criminal about the couple, Barnevernet gave the excuse that if allowed to see their children, Natalya and Zygys might kidnap them.[49] This one of the most twisted statements one could contrive, as it is actually Barnevernet who is guilty of kidnapping in most cases. On the contrary, any well-meaning parent would be within their human rights to protect their children by whatever means necessary, including rescue, if such a plan could be carried out.

---

49. Shutakova, N. (2020, February 28), (J. V. Maren, Interviewer).

Spring and Summer
2020

O n March 14, 2020, someone named Michael Snow published an online petition directed to US Senator David Purdue from Georgia, urging him to request that the Department of State intervene and rescue the children. Containing sufficient information to accurately convey the details of the Shutakova family's plight, the petition is convincing and powerful. First, the petition establishes the illegitimacy of Barnevernet's claim to the children, based on the subjective assessment that the children's routine is not good enough to meet the government standard, whatever that may be. There has been no violence, negligence, or drug use in their biological home to warrant removal from their parents. The petition also notes that it is likely Barnevernet simply wants to maintain custody of the children long enough to sever the familial bonds between them and their parents "in order to get the children forcibly adopted by strangers." It concludes with a shocking statistic: "In the past, other countries have intervened on the behalf of their citizens who had children seized by Norway. These countries include Czech Republic, Romania, India, Poland, and others. But never the U. S. government."[50] It is unknown whether Senator Purdue ever responded.

Natalya and Zygys were looking forward to a court hearing in April 2020 when the COVID-19 pandemic arrived. Disappointingly, it was rescheduled for five months later, in September 2020.[51] In this case, the coronavirus was used as an excuse to disrupt a fair and necessary legal procedure where time is of the essence. Looking back, this does not come as a surprise, as corrupt government officials have used the pandemic as an excuse to disrupt countless significant events and milestones all over the world, most notably the US presidential election.

Sadly, Brigita was not allowed to celebrate her 12th birthday with her family on May 17,

---

50. Snow, M. (2020, March 14). Norway has seized these American kids, Citizen Go.

51. Shutakova, N. (2020, May 20), (E. Metaxas, Interviewer).

2020. Her mother, Natalya, however, found an ingenious way to make sure Brigita knew how much she is missed, loved, and celebrated. Natalya asked friends and family from all over the world to use "#brigita12" when wishing Brigita a happy birthday on social media. Brigita was able to find them online. Natalya also printed the wishes in a notebook, including photographs of Brigita, photographs of her friends and loved ones, hopeful notes of blessing and cheer, and details of Brigita's captivity to help raise awareness.[52] Sadly, Barnevernet confiscated the notebook after discovering something critical of their organization. Later in September, they used the notebook against Natalya in court.[53]

On May 18, 2020, the faith-based Eric Metaxas Show aired an interview with Natalya, during which she expresses regret for taking her children to Norway. Not unexpectedly, it seems those who are most willing to help are those who identify as Christians, including Metaxas and other interviewers, Step Up 4 Children's Rights, and Natalya's church, New Life Church of Atlanta. These faith-based organizations, among others,

52. Shutakova, N. (2020, May 20), (E. Metaxas, Interviewer).

53. Shutakova, N. (2020). (S. Harrell, Interviewer)

have persisted in their unrelenting efforts to rescue the Shutakova children by raising awareness, raising funds, and raising their hands in prayer.

The same day the Eric Metaxas interview aired, President Trump appointed former Georgia House Speaker Mark Burkhalter to serve as US ambassador to Norway.[54] With strong ties to both Atlanta and Norway, Burkhalter is perfectly situated to help the Shutakova family. However, Natalya also makes it clear that the US government refuses to step in: "I've written letters to President Trump, I've written letters to my local senator, governor, and there's not much they can do. They say because this is not parental abduction, this is a state abduction…How can they not save innocent children, we have a lot of family in the states, good working Christians."[55] Others in support of the family have also written letters to the White House, Secretary of State Mike Pompeo, and Chief Counsel Richard T. Philips from the US Embassy in Oslo. Philips responded that he would not intervene.[56]

---

54. Garza, V. (2020, May 18). Trump Has Appointed a New Ambassador to Norway, *Norway Today*.

55. Shutakova, N. (2020, May 20), (E. Metaxas, Interviewer).

56. Step Up 4 Children's Rights, Facebook (2020, August 31)..

May 20, 2020 marked exactly one year since the Shutakova children were kidnapped. Natalya, Step Up 4 Children's Rights, and CitizenGO Deutsch organized a prayer event online on that day inviting people to pray for the Shutakova family:

> Pray for a quick reunification of this precious family and invite others to do so as well… pray that God would touch and heal their broken hearts, pray for the officials in Norway to release the children, pray for the US state department to speak up for their citizens, pray for the home church of this family to get involved and to speak up according to Proverbs 31:8, pray for media to cover this case on TV, radio, Internet...etc., and pray for the Norwegian "Barnevernet" system to be renewed so that children would no longer have to suffer.[57]

Amazingly, like an answer to those prayers, Natalya and Zygys were permitted to meet with the birthday girl, Brigita, on May 29, 2020. In Natalya's words, the meeting was

---

57. Step Up 4 Children's Rights and CitizenGO Deutsch, Facebook (2020, May 20).

"better late than never. (Brigita) was excited to spend time alone with her parents…and is very much looking to come back home." Several days after meeting with Brigita, Natalya and Zygys were permitted to meet with just Nikita on June 5, 2020, then with just Elizabeth on June 12, 2020.[58]

On June 18, 2020, Step Up 4 Children's Rights, along with others, held a protest of Barnevarnet outside the Norwegian Embassy in Vienna, Austria. Demonstrators carried signs demanding that "Norway, Return the American Kids." Bjorn Korf of Step Up 4 Children's Rights, and Maurius Reikeras, Norwegian human rights counsel, voiced their concerns directly to the Ambassador of the Royal Norwegian Embassy, Kjersti Ertresvaag Andersen. They also delivered a letter to him to deliver to Norway's Prime Minister, Kjell Ingolf Ropstad.[59] Included in the letter was a description of the atrocities perpetrated by Barnevernet against the Shutakova family up to that point, even recording the name of the Barnevernet caseworker responsible, Annette Fillingsnes. The letter also includes a plea to urge "Minister

58. Shutakova, N. (2020). (S. Harrell, Interviewer)

59. Step Up 4 Children's Rights, Facebook (2020, June 19).

Kjell Ingolf Ropstad to…hold Barnevernet at Nottodden Kommune accountable for their wrongful actions and for violating the rights of those children."[60]

The Shutakova children's last day of school for the year is June 19, 2020, the day after Vienna protest. Barnevernet decides for the family that it is better for the children to be with their friends on this day, rather than with their parents, against the children's wishes.[61] Less than two weeks later, on July 31st, 2020, Natalya and Zygys are permitted to meet with all three children, with the Shutakova's psychologist present.[62] The agency seems to make its decisions on a whim, with no rhyme or reason regarding what fates they decide for the children in their captivity.

60. Korf, B., Ledochowski, J., Prols, E., Norway, Return the American Kids

61. Shutakova, N. (2020). (S. Harrell, Interviewer).

62. Shutakova, N. (2020). (S. Harrell, Interviewer).

Fall and Winter 2020-2021

T he Shutakovas endured five consecutive days of Norwegian custody court from September 7th-11th, 2020. Natalya urged her followers on social media to pray for her family, demonstrating her unshakable faith in the Lord and His justice. Representatives from the U.S. Consulate and Lithuanian Embassy were present during the proceedings, giving hope to the victims. On the last day of court, Natalya and Zygys were instructed to wait three weeks for a decision regarding the fate of their children.[63]

> I know that all three children were speaking separately to the three judges, and they said they want to go home to mom and dad. Brigita said to judge that her foster family talks "trash" about my parents. Nikita said

63. Shutakova, N. (2020). (S. Harrell, Interviewer)

he cries every night because he doesn't want to be there. Liza (Elizabeth) misses hugs and kisses from us, but this is just small things I remember. I was crying when judge read out the things kids said, my heart was crying, even my husband was seen wiping tears off. It's such an emotional period that only God can heal. When you are hearing straight lies about yourself and manage to keep yourself under control, not show them you are furious and outrageous, you can only do it with the help of God. When your ego wants (you) to scream, "Are you done with your lies?" I just ask myself, "How would God like it if I were showing off my ego?"[64]

Sadly, after patiently waiting for three weeks on the court's decision, the Shutakovas learned on September 25th that they lost and would not regain custody of their children. The court gave them only five visits per year. While heartbreaking, it is expected for the victim families of Barneverent to lose and be discredited in court, over and over, until they're emotionally and financially exhausted. On

64. Shutakova, N. (2020). (S. Harrell, Interviewer)

October 8, 2020, Barnevernet added insult to injury by requiring Natalya to meet with one of their caseworkers to give Nikita a gift for his 11th birthday.

Natalya and Zygys concluded the court did not listen to them and had their attorney appeal to a higher court. The appeal was accepted in Lagmannsrett due to "great weaknesses in the previous verdict" and scheduled for June 2021. Only five percent of cases make it to this higher court, which will be a "fresh start," according to Natalya. She believes, and rightly so, that "God is moving things around" for her family. Already she and Zygys are preparing for their next day in court. They've accepted help, at no charge to them, from a government-appointed therapist whose positive feedback will be of great help in court. The court will also appoint a specialist to examine all family members and evaluate Natalya and Zygys' "abilities to take care of each child's needs."[65]

In December 2020, Natalya and Zygys were allowed to see each of their children once and exchange gifts. They met with Brigita on the 9th, then with Elizabeth and Nikita on the 18th. Natalya has more confidence in the girls'

---

65. Shutakova, N. (2020). (S. Harrell, Interviewer)

wellbeing than in Nikita's: "I am confident to say that girls are doing ok, but I cannot say that about my son he has the worst (foster) family now, they couldn't care less about his wellbeing, emotionally, especially. He has always been a very sensitive boy, but now that I saw him, he kept talking negative things about the family he lives in, I haven't heard one positive thing." His behavior while opening gifts was particularly concerning for Natalya, as he would rush to open them as if he were afraid someone would snatch them away. She believes his foster family takes things from him and is otherwise generally abusive toward him. Brigita attempts to contact her parents through social media but has not been successful other than to enter the occasional incorrect password for her parents' accounts.[66]

In January of 2021, like a beacon of good hope for the new year, the Shutakovas' attorney notified them that the government office overseeing Barnevernet, called Fylkesmannen, has opened an investigation against the local Barnevernet office in Notodden. These are the ones responsible for the horror the Shutakovas have endured. As a result of the investigation, Barnevernet's violations are surfacing,

---

66. Shutakova, N. (2020). (S. Harrell, Interviewer).

and their abuses are finally coming to light, according to Natalya, "So when the court finds out about this, its gonna put them in hot water, the court will see how they treated parents, never worked with them, never intended to reunify family."[67]

As in the Song of Songs, springtime brought forth a "new day of destiny" and "the early signs of (His) plans and purposes" (Song of Songs 2:13 TPT) for the Shutakova family. With the changing of the seasons, the family immediately began enjoying increased visitations thanks to the requests made by a court-appointed specialist who needed the extra time to observe the family together prior to the next court date in June 2021. In March 2021, just four days after Natalya's birthday, God blessed her and Zygys with a reunion with their two eldest children on March 5th. On March 26th, the couple met with Nikita and Elizabeth separately, for two hours each. On April 19th, Brigita enjoyed an outing to Kiste-fos Museum with her parents, then on April 23rd, Natalya and Zygys enjoyed a visit with the younger children. For Natalya, these brief meetings are a bittersweet blessing: "For me, these days are always hard, stressful because

---

67. Shutakova, N. (2021). (S. Harrell, Interviewer).

of (the) emotional rollercoaster. Long drives, hellos, and goodbyes."[68] For a temporary time, it may seem evil has prevailed in the case of the Shutakova family; however, we can rest assured that the Lord Jesus already sees their victorious outcome in this trial and is cheering them through the home stretch: "A thief has only one thing in mind—he wants to steal, slaughter, and destroy. But I have come to give you everything in abundance, more than you expect—life in its fullness until you overflow" (John 10:10 TPT). Please keep the Shutakova family in your prayers until they are permanently reunited.

First visitation after split up, ages 11, 9, and 6.

68. Shutakova, N. (2021). (S. Harrell, Interviewer).

Epilogue

Natalya and her family endured another custody court date on June 17, 2021. One week prior to that date, she lamented, "Now that Trump is out of the office, the US Embassy won't even attend court this time. How sad. They lost interest all of a sudden."[69] However, one week after court, on June 24, 2021, her outlook was more hopeful. She shared that their lawyer believes their youngest, Elizabeth, has a good chance of coming home, and Nikita has a 50% chance. Both children confirmed for the judge that they would like to return home to their parents. Regaining custody of their eldest, Brigita, is proving more challenging, according to Natalya, "When it comes to Brigita we might have to send another claim to court for her. She's most difficult because she's thirteen and that behavior is unstable….We have 4 weeks waiting praying time."[70]

69. Shutakova, N. (2021). (S. Harrell, Interviewer)

70. Shutakova, N. (2021). (S. Harrell, Interviewer).

Late in the evening of September 2, 2021, the Shutakovas received the court's decision. The youngest at nine years old, Elizabeth, was returned to Natalya and Zygys a month later on October 9th. With their son Nikita, the couple will be allowed ten unsupervised, weekend-long sleepover visits per year at home. For the time being, their eldest child, Brigita, will only be allowed to visit her parents five times per year in a supervised setting.

Of the decision, Natalya says it is a great start and she is beyond thankful to God. It has been two long years since her children were kidnapped. Their attorney added that she has not seen such a long, forty-page decision in her entire career.[71] Let all who read this story recognize God's sovereignty is as He steadily delivers the Shutakova children from captivity.

> Little children, you can be certain that you belong to God and have conquered them, for the One who is living in you is far greater than the one who is in the world. (1 John 4:4 TPT)

71. Shutakova, N. (2021). (S. Harrell, Interviewer)

How You Can Help

T he Shutakova family was not financially prepared for the expenses associated with defending themselves against the Norwegian government, whose resources are seemingly endless. The family must consult regularly with various professionals to navigate the legal process of regaining child custody.

Please help them bring Brigita and Nikita back home with this online Christian fundraising link. The funds go directly to their family. May God bless your compassion and generosity!

https://www.givesendgo.com/G2AUQ

Other Books by the Author

His Child: Asking Jesus for Your True Identity

His Child is a collection of sixty devotions showcasing real-life examples of God's unconditional love woven throughout the author's life. God's redemptive work is beautifully illustrated through short stories from her journey, meaningful Scriptures and quotes, and guided prayers to encourage your communication with Jesus.

Works Cited

1) Flory, N. (2019, October 10). The American-Born Kidnapped Children of Norway . Retrieved from The Stream: https://stream.org/the-american-born-kidnapped-children-of-norway/?fbclid=IwAR2Yxj5_tBl7ByHAoa5T8TXLcZIAtDeVwBe-Klf111uvh-P5vZhOiAo3MFVs

2) Givetash, L. (2019, August 3). A$AP Rocky Released from Swedish Jail, Back in the US. Retrieved from NBC News: https://www.nbcnews.com/news/world/u-s-warned-sweden-negative-consequences-if-asap-rocky-wasn-n1038961?fbclid=IwAR-251IF4V0zyjJjFf96ZTvePO9eezZ0roidqEgK_yHx-67iuBnxj3aXTou7k

3) Hurd, D. (2019, July 17). Norwegian Nightmare: 'Barnevernet' Preys On Children and Parents. Retrieved from CBN News: https://www1.cbn.com/cbnnews/world/2019/july/norwegian-nightmare-barnevernet-preys-on-children-and-parents-nbsp?nocache=1&fbclid=IwAR29MgvsNSFQrztlMqFsU-9VDXet6nbtkPTMlzT5gl0mfX6jVb12MviKGIro

4) Hurd, D. (2019, September 27). 'Our Hearts Are Shattered': Norway Takes Permanent Custody of 3 American Children from Christian Parents. Retrieved from CBN News: https://www1.cbn.com/cbnnews/cwn/2019/september/our-hearts-are-shattered-norway-takes-permanent-custody-of-3-american-children-from-christian-parents

5) International Protest: "STOP Barnevernet Ideology" in child protection laws. (2019, September 4). Retrieved from Family News: https://familynews.ro/international-protest-stop-barnevernet-ideology-in-child-protection-laws/

6) Judson, J. (2018, April 12). US, Norway officially enter arrangement to share supplies for national security. Retrieved from Defense News: https://www.defensenews.com/land/2018/04/12/us-norway-officially-enter-arrangement-to-share-supplies-for-national-security/?fbclid=IwAR2femAX-Lzdu4RqoNtt039u2zxcNk6bK3PFMqoJ3fcxxM-vsm-nVCilNjrtM

7) Kay, L. J. (2020, April 14). Don't Wait to Report a Missing Person. Retrieved from The Enterprise: https://www.springhopeenterprise.com/stories/dont-wait-to-report-a-missing-person,206182

8) Korf, B. (2019, November 6). Open Letter to the US Embassy in Oslo. Retrieved from Step Up 4 Children's Rights: https://stepup4childrensrights.com/open-letter-to-us-embassy/?fbclid=IwAR3xLAh-pib_uPPvmoigSm_7Cl34-NexSWCY_QdwhAaKKw-Gy1zUJQMAQV2w

9) Korf, B. (2019, June 13). Three American children brutally ripped from their beds at night in Norway. Retrieved from Step Up 4 Children's Rights: https://stepup4childrensrights.com/three-american-children/?fbclid=IwAR24K3mTOF9PADYd5rfDW-me0M0CVUaKqSXI07EE3ExvVEtD1OBaPzsoqmrg

10) Bonanza Media. (Director). (2019). American Children Lost to Norway [Motion Picture].

11) Miltimore, J. (2020, September 24). Black Lives Matter's Goal to 'Disrupt' the Nuclear Family Fits a Marxist Aim That Goes Back a Century and a Half. Retrieved from FEE: https://fee.org/articles/black-lives-matter-s-goal-to-disrupt-the-nuclear-family-fits-a-marxist-aim-that-goes-back-a-century-and-a-half/

12) More than a National Day: Understanding May 17th of Norway. (n.d.). Retrieved from The Nordic Page: https://www.tnp.no/norway/exclusive/2280-norway-more-than-a-national-day-understanding-may-17th

13) Shutakova, N. (2019, June 6). Podcast Episode 14 - Three American Children Brutally Taken by Norway's Dysfunctional CPS. (B. Korf, Interviewer) Step Up 4 Children's Rights.

14) Shutakova, N. (2020). (S. Harrell, Interviewer)

15) Shutakova, N. (2020, May 20). Natalya Shutakova - An Update On Norway Child Protective Services Nightmare. (E. Metaxas, Interviewer)

16) Shutakova, N. (2020, February 15). Norway Seized Our Kids. (B. Korf, Interviewer)

17) Shutakova, N. (2020, February 28). US mom begs Trump to help free her children kidnapped by Norway's child protective services. (J. V. Maren, Interviewer)

18) Smith, S. (2019, July 3). 3 American children removed from parents' home by Norway's child services. Retrieved from The Christian Post: https://www.christianpost.com/news/3-american-children-removed-from-parents-home-by-norways-child-services-231913/?fbclid=IwAR33ajv_dZo_61ZSKHOuagM0Cv_Amup0MbG_6pvEnwk8xzLn3AgTriGz-CM

19) Smith, S. (2019, October 5). Norway refuses to reunite mother with son despite victory at top European court. Retrieved from The Christian Post: https://www.christianpost.com/news/norway-refuses-to-reunite-mother-with-son-despite-victory-at-top-european-court.html

20) Smith, S. (2019, August 10). Norwegian police drop criminal case against US family, but kids remain in CPS custody. Retrieved from The Christian Post: https://www.christianpost.com/news/norwegian-police-drop-criminal-case-against-us-family-but-kids-remain-in-cps-custody-232462/?fbclid=IwAR3_myA_SJSeTVINYnO5QJ3cb_QOm6eReaY-hABrN-kKACzxwFdspi_cR5Rc

21) Snow, M. (2020, March 14). Norway has seized these American kids. Help rescue Elizabeth, Nikita, and

Brigita! Retrieved from Citizen Go: https://citizengo.org/en/177592-we-ask-united-states-senator-david-purdue-request-department-state-protest-seizing-three?m=7&tcid=71635320&utm_campaign=

22) Garza, V. (2020, May 18). Trump Has Appointed a New Ambassador to Norway. Retrieved from Norway Today: https://norwaytoday.info/news/trump-has-appointed-a-new-ambassador-to-norway/

23) Step Up 4 Children's Rights and CitizenGO Deutsch. (2020, May 20). Global Day of Prayer Event. Retrieved from Facebook: https://www.facebook.com/events/702059357210104

24) Korf, B., Ledochowski, J., Prols, E. (2020, June 19). Norway, Return the American Kids - Open Letter to the Norwegian Embassy in Vienna, Austria. Retrieved from Step Up 4 Children's Rights: https://stepup4childrensrights.com/openletter2020-06/?fbclid=IwAR1mNZR7vT41EsV9_kwBqXVsPza7vICer-EFFNSB2jXVe56XMGc91mLIFWZ4

25) Step Up 4 Children's Rights. (2020, June 19). Retrieved from Facebook: https://www.facebook.com/StepUp4ChildrensRights/posts/1626845187478868

26) Step Up 4 Children's Rights. (2020, August 31). Retrieved from Facebook: https://www.facebook.com/StepUp4ChildrensRights/photos/a.695074137322649/1691127861050600/

27) Shutakova, N. (2021). (S. Harrell, Interviewer)